21 days to spring

AF624542

Stephanie Agotborde

BookLeaf Publishing

Presentation by *BookLeaf Publishing*

Web: www.bookleafpub.com

E-mail: info@bookleafpub.com

ISBN: 9789357445627

First edition 2022

DEDICATION

To the universe, for always having my back.

ACKNOWLEDGE MENT

I want to thank my sister for inspiring and supporting me with her visual art.
And all my friends that have been there, bringing joy in the darkest times.

September 1st

21 days of hope
while spring comes
Though my body is physically in the north
hemisphere
I was born in the south.

And I can feel how this caterpillar
In my heart
Wants to fly

Winter can be
Very long for the heart.

Dear,
When nothing is wrong outside
But the wound bleeds from the inside
What is left to do?

Pick up the pieces,
Hold yourself together
Pray for your soul

Stay at home
Water the plants
Watch the cats grow old

Maybe, eventually
You'll find the strength
To let some art out

21 days of hope
Let it bloom

It can always be spring in September
It just depends
Where you are looking at the seasons from

On Freedom

I've realised today
That mind freedom is just
A state in a
Moment

At any time
You can open that door
In your head

Try -
Close your eyes
And be present

If you get to feel it
Then it's real

More than trying -

Claim it

An oasis in the dessert

The dessert
A dark tunnel
The emptiness
Of not finding

Joy
Peace
Happiness

It can take
So many forms

Sickness
Depression
Lost

But

The chaos
The silence
The confusion

Couldn’t exist
Without their opposites

Counterbalance

Do you still remember
How to swing?
You only have to pull yourself
To get to the other side

Flow to balance
Flow to stillness
Flow to get through

Close your eyes
Feel the wind
And just
Connect

Manifest your river

I don't need anyone to save me

No one can
Know my demons as I do
Or know
When I'm ready

When I was 7 years old
I loved the sea
And it loved me back as well
So much that
I almost drowned with my dad
In the waters of Praia Brava, in Brasil

For many years I thought
He had pulled me out

23 years afterwards I discovered
He didn't
He couldn't
We were too far away from each other

He just talked to me
And I made the choice

To stay on this earth
For longer

The final choice
In most cases -
is always ours

Surround yourself with people
In your same or a higher frequency
And they will uplift you
By simply being

Save yourself
Discover your power

A little trick:
Don’t forget to smile

Joy is like freedom

A moment
A second
A smile

Coffee in the mornings
Waking up with a loved one
(Either human or cat)

If we can acknowledge how
Impermanent each moment is
And just be present
Fully present

That's the closest to living high

On mistakes

I don't care so much
About the opportunities I didn't take
Or the relationships
That went downhill

What really hurts
Is all the times I fucked up
The relationship with myself

All the times that I
Placed myself and my needs
Second, or third

Every time I betrayed
My own heart

I have dozens of excuses
But I can also
Forgive myself

The hard thing to know
Is how to move forward

I'm healing
Everyday

I trust myself now

But I don’t fully know
Who I am

I have the power
To not hurt myself again
But I can’t seem to be able
To grab it

And it’s Saturday night
My head feels so heavy

I just miss having
A meaningful conversation
And the thrill
Of something real

Existence is meant
to be enjoyed

A recipe for New Moons

Face your demons
Grab your power
Speak your truth

Sleep under the stars
Fly far and
Sometimes call back home

Look at your wildest dreams
and turn them into
Motion

You deserve it

On festivals & Love

I'm still a bit high
Dance and music brings
So many nice memories
So much empowering

But the most lovely thing
Happened this time
A random guy told me

"You look like love
Oh, so beautiful"

And I don't give a damn
How high he was too
Because either way
He was hell right

So I put myself to sleep
Thinking about that
Repeating that phrase

Like a new mantra

Trying to immortalise the feeling
Of hearing the most moving thing

Anyone has ever told me

And I'm so grateful,
Lovely stranger
Because now I feel I have
Something to aspire
And live for

Breathe in 4, exhale in 8

As I sit in nature
And try to be still

My mind flies
To multiple spaces and
Parallel times

In a way we can be
In different places at the same time

As my thoughts rush
My body feels sick

Slow down hun
That's all you need

That's one key
To feel lightness
Less things
Dragging you down

Heaven on earth

Exists but
Can only be real
Here and now

9/9

Portal days
Are for
Revelations

And revelations
Are not always fun

There's nothing to fix
Sometimes
And all that is left is
Acceptance

In the end
You just have to

Let yourself be
Love yourself
And be kind

Unconditionally

Contemplations

My lovers fall
like autumn leaves

Enough

Stop with so many questions
Or trying to understand
And know
Or even heal
Everything

One step at a time

All this journey
Is connected
But it's not
A goddamn
Checklist

You are not
A Trello board
And some things
Are just messy

Believe
All will fall
Into place

Believe in you
Trust that curiosity

Because it will take you
Closer
To your heart
And becoming
Who you really
Are

No judgements
No hurries

Inner spring

My spirit lifts
Under the sun

Soon I
become
The sun

All the questions
In the universe
Fade

And I can just feel
All the comfort
In the
Unknown

I can laugh
At my
Darkness

And dance
With all my
Demons

Life becomes

Pure
Without all the
Fear

As I embrace
The magic
In the mystery of
Existence

No matter
How dark
It might get

On flowers

How many parts
Of ourselves
We might end up denying
To survive

I was born as a female
Identified as a woman
In a world rule by men

I'm not sure
At this point
At 30 years old

How much of myself
did I bury?

The divine feminity
Flowers in spring
Intuitive gifts

My own body

For the sake of not looking
Weak
or being

Ashamed
or even
Abused

We do what we have to do
To protect ourselves

But this is
It

I give myself
the right of
Being

Because no one else will

Lights on

I can't sleep
With the lights off
Again

The fear
Is real
Even if the ghosts
Are not

There's enough darkness already
Don't let me get started
There's not much to do about it

Sometimes
The cards
Play this game
And we have to lose
To win again

I feel sick and tired
While hopeful and all shiny

I'm all
At the same
Time

Wholeness
Is the prize
But it also comes
With a price

Can I
Take it back?

Or

Can I
Be brave enough?

The dices
Unexpectedly
Turned

There's another game
And here we go again

The ocean is so far away today
The sun and the beach
Are only
In my heart
And behind
My eyes

Will happiness

come back?

Poetry as a weapon

Leaves dance
Like my feelings

There are moments for everything
The seasons flow
The sunrise always comes with a sunset

And my poems are the living evidence
Of impermanence

The only way to hold on
Is making it words
Although it is also
A way to leave it all behind

The sand escapes from us all

So I immortalise all with passion
In language
In culture
Like a desperate cry

Because beauty needs to remain

My resistance to accept
that you can’t live
high from whatever
your drug is
Gets hold of me

But the shadows are there for a reason

To manifest a different reality
Is to break an egg

Rebirth

As below
So above

The sounds come in
And the serpent
Takes over
My surrender body

The drums
Lead my way
To this portal

And I close my eyes and I
Begin to see

The waterfall
Falling over
My naked body

The fire
The sacred
They key
To the secret of creation

To my feminine power

Fearless in my heart
I open the door
To let it all
Out:

Fear
Guilt
And
Shame

Because I repressed
Being a woman
For so long
To protect myself

I clean
I heal
With love

All my female ancestors
Shower me with
Golden and red sparks

And as I shine
My heart
Opens its way to a
Rose

This is how
I finally bloom

As above
So below

On Inertia

Don't hide yourself
from writing
Under this ocean of
tears

Take that sadness
Out and just
Throw it

At everything
That is
Blank

The only way to
To leave, for real
Is building that bridge
To walk to the other side

Above your misery

Can't you see?

Writing
Will
Save

You

Hiding your gifts
Is only a highway
To neurosis

Here and now

I'm being borned
Again

After all these darkness
I can see the flames

The sun is out
I'm filled with this peace

Nothing more pure

No fear
No anxiety

And no drugs

All is
Where's it's supposed to
Be

I belong

As I see a plane
And for the first time
I don't want to jump in it

I’m fine here
I’m where I’m supposed to be

I’m not afraid
To believe in myself
anymore

Sunshine

I thought I should write
Something
A bit less heavy

I mean, it's September
No one should live
This heavy

Time off
A cigarette on

Write something like
A butterfly
Blooming trees
Or just
The dancing of the leaves

But it seems
I wear sunglasses
And I just
Can't

Spring is in the air
Smoke in my lungs
In my heart I feel

I am the sun

But this sun
Burns

Happy full moon

The moon
is out
- It's full

The sky feels
like home

I'm present
Under her precious light

And for a moment
There's no more darkness

www.ingramcontent.com/pod-product-compliance
Lightning Source LLC
Chambersburg PA
CBHW051743130826
49812CB00033B/983
9789357445627